TREATS

just great recipes

GENERAL INFORMATION

The level of difficulty of the recipes in this book
is expressed as a number from 1 (simple) to 3 (difficult).

TREATS
just great recipes
baked pasta

McRae BOOKS

SERVES 4–6

PREPARATION 30 min + 1 h to drain

COOKING 1 h 15 min

DIFFICULTY level 1

Baked Spaghetti
with tomato sauce

Tomato sauce: Cook the tomatoes with $^1/_2$ teaspoon salt in a covered saucepan over medium heat for 5 minutes. • Transfer to a colander with large holes and let drain for 1 hour. • Return to the saucepan and add the onion, garlic, basil, oil, sugar, and salt. Cover and bring to a boil over medium heat. Simmer for about 40 minutes, or until the sauce has thickened. • Remove from the heat and run through a food mill or process in a food processor until smooth. • Preheat the oven to 350°F (180°C/gas 4). • Butter a large baking dish. • Cook the spaghetti in a large pan of salted, boiling water for just over half the time indicated on the package. • Drain the spaghetti and placed in the prepared dish. • Spoon the tomato sauce over the top. Sprinkle with the Parmesan and oregano. • Bake for about 25 minutes, or until the cheese is golden brown. Serve hot.

Tomato Sauce
3 lb (1.5 kg) tomatoes, coarsely chopped
Salt
1 red onion, thinly sliced
2 cloves garlic, finely chopped
Leaves from 1 small bunch fresh basil, torn
2 tablespoons extra-virgin olive oil
$^1/_2$ teaspoon sugar

1 lb (500 g) spaghetti
1 cup (125 g) freshly grated Parmesan cheese
1 teaspoon dried oregano

Baked Pasta
with potatoes and tomatoes

Preheat the oven to 350°F (180°C/gas 4). • Blanch the tomatoes in a large pan of boiling water for 1 minute, then place under cold running water. Slip off the skins and chop the flesh finely. Place in a bowl with the basil and season with salt and pepper. • Peel the potatoes and cut into ¼-inch (5-mm) thick slices. • Grease an ovenproof dish with a little of the oil. Place a layer of tomato on the bottom and cover with a layer of raw pasta, followed by layers of potatoes, olives, onion, oil, cheese, and oregano. • Sprinkle with the bread crumbs and drizzle with the remaining oil. • Bake until the potatoes and pasta are tender, about 1 hour. Serve hot.

3 lb (1.5 kg) firm ripe tomatoes
10 fresh basil leaves, torn
Salt and freshly ground black pepper
1 lb (500 g) potatoes
½ cup (125 ml) extra-virgin olive oil
1 lb (500 g) short pasta shape
    such as penne or conchiglie
1 cup (100 g) black olives, pitted
    and thinly sliced
1 large onion, thinly sliced
1 cup (125 g) freshly grated pecorino
    cheese
1 tablespoon finely chopped fresh
    oregano
½ cup (75 g) fine dry bread crumbs

SERVES 6–8

PREPARATION 45 min + 1 h to soak

COOKING 3 h

DIFFICULTY level 2

Baked Pasta
with eggplant and meat sauce

Soak the eggplant in a large bowl of salted cold water for 1 hour. • Meat Sauce: Sauté the beef and onion in the extra-virgin oil in a medium saucepan over high heat until browned, about 10 minutes. • Add the wine, tomatoes, tomato paste, cinnamon stick, clove, basil, and oregano. Season with salt and pepper. Simmer for 2 hours, adding water or stock if the sauce sticks to the pan. Discard the cinnamon and clove. • Drain the eggplant and pat dry on paper towels. • Heat the frying oil in a large deep frying pan until very hot. Fry the eggplant in batches for 5–7 minutes, or until tender. Drain on paper towels. • Cook the pasta in a large pot of salted boiling water for half the time indicated on the package. Drain well. • Preheat the oven to 350°F (180°C/gas 4). • Grease a baking dish with oil. • Toss the pasta with two-thirds of the meat sauce, the eggplant, and caciocavallo. • Beat the eggs with the pecorino until frothy. • Arrange half the pasta in the baking dish. Add the remaining meat sauce and arrange the hard-boiled eggs on top. Top with the remaining pasta. Pour the egg and pecorino mixture over the top. • Bake for 40–45 minutes, or until golden brown.

1 eggplant (aubergine), thinly sliced

Meat Sauce
1 lb (500 g) ground (minced) lean beef
1 large red onion, finely chopped
1/4 cup (60 ml) extra-virgin olive oil
1/3 cup (90 ml) dry red wine
2 lb (1 kg) tomatoes, peeled and finely chopped
1 tablespoon tomato paste (concentrate)
1 stick cinnamon
1 clove
Leaves from 1 small bunch basil, torn
1/2 teaspoon dried oregano
Salt and freshly ground black pepper
Water or stock (optional)
1 cup (250 ml) olive oil, for frying
1 lb (500 g) dried small short pasta, such as anellini (small pasta rings)
3 oz (90 g) caciocavallo or ricotta salata cheese, cut into small cubes
2 large eggs, lightly beaten
2 hard-boiled eggs, thinly sliced
1/2 cup (60 g) freshly grated pecorino cheese

SERVES 6–8

PREPARATION 1 h

COOKING 1 h 20 min

DIFFICULTY level 2

Baked Pasta
stuffed with vegetables

Heat the butter and oil in a large frying pan over medium heat and sauté the onion until softened, 3–4 minutes. • Add the zucchini, carrots, broccoli, and green beans and sauté for 7–8 minutes. • Add the water and season with salt and pepper. Cover and simmer over low heat for 20 minutes. • Béchamel Sauce: Heat the milk in a saucepan over low heat. Remove from the heat just before it begins to boil. • Melt the butter in a medium saucepan over low heat. • Add the flour and stir with a wooden spoon. • Remove from the heat and add ¼ cup (60 ml) of the hot milk. Beat well with a whisk to prevent lumps from forming. • Gradually pour in the remaining milk, whisking constantly. • Return to the heat and bring to a boil over low heat. Cook for about 5 minutes, stirring constantly, until the sauce has thickened. • Remove from the heat. Season with nutmeg and salt. • When the vegetables are almost ready, uncover the pan so that all the liquid cooks off. • Remove from the heat and stir in the Gruyière and a ladleful of Béchamel sauce. • Preheat the oven to 350°F (180°C/gas 4) • Butter a large baking dish. • Cook the giant conchiglie in a large pan of salted, boiling water for half the time indicated on the package. • Drain well and let cool a little. • Fill the conchiglie with the vegetables and arrange in the baking dish. Cover with the remaining Béchamel and the tomatoes. Sprinkle with the Parmesan. • Bake for about 20 minutes, or until golden brown. Serve hot.

2 tablespoons butter
2 tablespoons extra-virgin olive oil
3 zucchini (courgettes), diced
2 carrots, diced
1 lb (500 g) broccoletti
10 oz (300 g) French beans
    (green beans), diced
½ cup (125 ml) water
Salt and freshly ground black pepper
1 small onion, diced
8 oz (250 g) Gruyière (Swiss) cheese,
    chopped
About 24 giant conchiglie or other
    large, hollow dried pasta shape
4 oz (125 g) chopped tomatoes

Béchamel Sauce
2 cups (500 ml) milk
3 tablespoons butter
⅓ cup (50 g) all-purpose (plain) flour
Nutmeg

1 cup (125 g) freshly grated Parmesan
    cheese

SERVES 4

PREPARATION 15 min

COOKING 30 min

DIFFICULTY level 1

Baked Rigatoni
with mortadella

Preheat the oven to 400°F (200°C/gas 6). • Butter a large baking dish. • Mix the mortadella and cheese with the cream and ¼ cup (30 g) of Parmesan in a large bowl. • Cook the pasta in a large pan of salted, boiling water for half the time indicated on the package. Drain and transfer to the bowl. Season with salt and pepper. Mix well and transfer to the prepared dish. • Sprinkle with the remaining Parmesan. • Bake for 15–20 minutes, or until a golden crust forms on the surface. Serve hot.

8 oz (250 g) mortadella, cut into small cubes

2 oz (60 g) Gruyière (Swiss) cheese, cut into small cubes

¾ cup (200 ml) heavy (double) cream

¾ cup (90 g) freshly grated Parmesan cheese

12 oz (350 g) rigatoni

Salt and freshly ground black pepper

SERVES 4–6

PREPARATION 20 min

COOKING 45 min

DIFFICULTY level 1

Baked Tagliatelle
with ham and mushrooms

Preheat the oven to 375°F (190°C/gas 5). • Butter a large baking dish. • Cook the tagliatelle for half the time indicated on the package. • Sauté the prosciutto in the butter in a large frying pan over medium heat for 5 minutes. • Drain the mushrooms, reserving the water. Chop coarsely and add to the prosciutto. • Simmer over medium heat for 6–7 minutes, or until the mushrooms are tender, adding the reserved water. Season with salt and pepper. • Add the pasta and mix in almost all the Béchamel and 3 tablespoons of Parmesan. • Place in the baking dish and spread with the remaining Béchamel. Sprinkle with the remaining Parmesan. • Bake for 30–35 minutes, or until golden brown. Serve hot.

14 oz (400 g) dried spinach tagliatelle
½ cup (60 g) prosciutto (Parma ham), finely chopped
¼ cup (60 g) butter
2 oz (60 g) dried mushrooms, soaked in warm water for 15 minutes
Salt and freshly ground white pepper
1 quantity Béchamel Sauce (see page 8)
½ cup (60 g) freshly grated Parmesan cheese

Baked Tagliatelle
with tomatoes and mozzarella

Sauté the onion, celery, and parsley in the oil in a large frying pan over medium heat for 5 minutes. • Add the tomatoes and season with salt and pepper. • Reduce the heat, partially cover, and simmer for 30 minutes. • Preheat the oven to 400°F (200°C/ gas 6). • Butter a large baking dish. • Place a layer of tomato sauce in the bottom of the dish. Cover with the tagliatelle. Top with the remaining sauce, followed by the mozzarella. Sprinkle with the Parmesan. • Bake for about 25 minutes, or until golden brown on top. • Serve hot.

1 onion, finely chopped

1 small stick celery, finely chopped

2 tablespoons finely chopped fresh parsley

1/3 cup (90 ml) extra-virgin olive oil

1 lb (500 g) tomatoes, peeled and chopped

Salt and freshly ground black pepper

1 lb (500 g) fresh tagliatelle

14 oz (400 g) mozzarella cheese, sliced

1 cup (125 g) freshly grated Parmesan cheese

SERVES 4–6

PREPARATION 40 min + 1 h to drain

COOKING 1 h

DIFFICULTY level 2

Baked Pasta

with eggplant

Place the eggplants in a colander. Sprinkle with the sea salt and let drain for 1 hour. • Beat the eggs and water in a small bowl. Use a balloon whisk to beat in the flour until smooth. • Rinse the eggplant well and dry with paper towels. • Dip the slices of eggplant into the egg mixture. • Heat the frying oil in a large frying pan and fry the eggplant in batches until golden brown on both sides. • Drain well on paper towels. • Heat the extra-virgin olive oil in a frying pan and sauté the onion until softened. • Stir in the tomatoes and parsley and season with salt. • Preheat the oven to 375°F (190°C/gas 5). • Butter a large baking dish. • Cook the pasta in a large pan of salted, boiling water until just al dente. • Drain and add to the pan with the sauce. • Sprinkle some of the pecorino cheese into a baking dish and top with a little tomato sauce. Spoon in a layer of the pasta, followed by layers of fried eggplants, pecorino, and tomato sauce. Repeat until all the ingredients are in the pan, finishing with a layer of tomato sauce. • Bake for 30 minutes. Serve hot.

2 medium eggplants (aubergines), thinly sliced
Coarse sea salt
2 large eggs
2 tablespoons cold water
$1/3$ cup (50 g) all-purpose (plain) flour
1 cup (250 ml) olive oil, for frying
$1/4$ cup (60 ml) extra-virgin olive oil
1 onion, finely chopped
3 cups (750 g) peeled and chopped tomatoes
1 bunch fresh parsley, finely chopped
Salt
12 oz (350 g) rigatoni
1 cup (125 g) freshly grated pecorino cheese

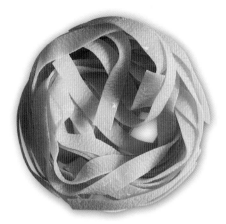

SERVES 4–6

PREPARATION 40 min

COOKING 55 min

DIFFICULTY level 2

Tagliatelle Mold
with peas

Melt 2 tablespoons of butter in a large frying pan over medium heat and sauté the scallions until softened. Add the prosciutto and sauté for 3 minutes. • Stir in the flour and pour in the milk. Cook over low heat for 5 minutes, stirring constantly. • Season with salt, stir in the Parmesan, and let cool. • Cook the peas in salted, boiling water for 10 minutes. • Drain and set aside. • Use a wooden spoon to mix in the egg yolks and about half the peas. • Beat the egg whites until stiff then fold them into the scallion mixture. • Preheat the oven to 400°F (200°C/gas 6). • Butter an 8-inch (20-cm) ring mold and sprinkle it with the bread crumbs. • Cook the pasta in a large pan of salted, boiling water until just al dente. • Drain well and add to the pan with the sauce. Spoon the pasta into the prepared pan. • Bake for 25 minutes. Melt the remaining butter in a large frying pan and sauté the peas for 3 minutes. • Invert the mold onto a serving platter and serve hot with the peas.

1/4 cup (60 ml) butter
4 scallions (spring onions,) finely chopped
3/4 cup (90 g) diced prosciutto (Parma ham)
2 tablespoons all-purpose (plain) flour
1 2/3 cups (400 ml) milk, warmed
Salt
1/2 cup (60 g) freshly grated Parmesan cheese
2 cups (300 g) peas
4 large eggs, separated
14 oz (400 g) tagliatelle

SERVES 4–6

PREPARATION 30 min

COOKING 45 min

DIFFICULTY level 2

Baked Rigatoni
with ham and mushrooms

Preheat the oven to 400°F (200°C/gas 6). • Butter a baking dish. • Mix half the Parmesan into the Béchamel. • Sauté the mushrooms in half the butter in a frying pan over medium heat for 8–10 minutes. • Add the ham and prosciutto and cook for 5 minutes. • Cook the pasta in a large pan of salted, boiling water until just al dente. • Drain and arrange half the pasta in the prepared dish. Top with half the mushrooms and ham. Cover with half of the Béchamel. Make a second layer with the pasta, mushrooms, ham, and Béchamel. Sprinkle with the remaining Parmesan and dot with the remaining butter. • Bake for 12–15 minutes, or until golden brown. • Serve hot.

½ cup (60 g) freshly grated Parmesan cheese

1 quantity Béchamel Sauce (see page 8)

8 oz (250 g) mushrooms, thinly sliced

¼ cup (60 g) butter

3 oz (90 g) ham, cut into thin strips

5 oz (150 g) prosciutto (Parma ham), cut into thin strips

1 lb (500 g) rigatoni

Baked Pasta
with cheese

SERVES 4–6
PREPARATION 15 min
COOKING 1 h
DIFFICULTY level 1

Preheat the oven to 400°F (200°C/gas 6). • Butter a large baking dish. • Cook the pasta in a large pot of salted boiling water with a drop of the oil for half the time indicated on the package. • Drain well and transfer to a large bowl. Drizzle with the remaining oil to prevent sticking. • Mix Béchamel into the pasta along with almost all of the pecorino. • Arrange a layer of pasta in the baking dish and cover with the Parmesan. Top with the remaining pasta and sprinkle with pecorino. Top with the remaining butter. • Bake for 40–45 minutes, or until the top is golden brown. Serve hot.

1 lb (500 g) short hollow dried pasta, such as macaroni or penne
2 tablespoons extra-virgin olive oil
1 quantity Béchamel Sauce (see page 8)
1/8 teaspoon freshly grated nutmeg
1 1/4 cups (150 g) freshly grated pecorino cheese
5 oz (150 g) Parmesan cheese, thinly sliced

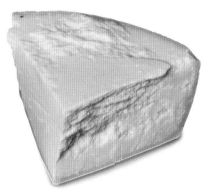

SERVES 4–6

PREPARATION 20 min

COOKING 30 min

DIFFICULTY level 1

Baked Tagliatelle
with eggs and parmesan

Prepare the Béchamel Sauce. Let cool a little then stir in the eggs and half the Parmesan. • Preheat the oven to 350°F (180°C/gas 4). • Butter a large baking dish. • Bring the vegetable stock to a boil and cook the tagliatelle in it for 1 minute. Drain well and add to the baking dish. • Spoon the Béchamel over the top. Sprinkle with the remaining Parmesan and dot with the butter. • Bake for 15–20 minutes, or until golden brown on top. • Let rest for 5 minutes before serving.

1 quantity Béchamel Sauce (see page 8)
3 large eggs, lightly beaten
1 cup (125 g) freshly grated Parmesan cheese
2 tablespoons butter
3 quarts (3 liters) Vegetable Stock
1 lb (500 g) tagliatelle

SERVES 4–6

PREPARATION 15 min

COOKING 30 min

DIFFICULTY level 1

Baked Pappardelle
with pumpkin

Preheat the oven to 400°F (200°C/gas 6). • Oil a large baking dish. • Sauté the pancetta and garlic in the oil in a large frying pan over medium heat until pale gold. • Add the pumpkin and wine and simmer for 10 minutes. • Cook the pasta in a large pot of salted boiling water until al dente, 3–5 minutes. • Drain and add to the pumpkin mixture. Simmer over medium heat for 2 minutes. • Add the parsley and season with pepper. Discard the garlic. • Transfer the mixture to the prepared dish. Top with the Fontina and butter. Sprinkle with the Parmesan. • Bake until lightly browned, 10–15 minutes. • Serve hot.

1 cup (125 g) diced pancetta or bacon
1 clove garlic, lightly crushed but whole
1/4 cup (60 ml) extra-virgin olive oil
8 oz (250 g) pumpkin flesh, thinly sliced
1/2 cup (125 ml) dry white wine
14 oz (400 g) fresh pappardelle
1 tablespoon finely chopped fresh parsley
Freshly ground black pepper
2 cups (250 g) freshly grated Fontina cheese
1 tablespoon butter
4 tablespoons freshly grated Parmesan cheese

Sicilian Timbale

Cook the asparagus, broccoli, and fennel separately in salted boiling water until tender, 5–7 minutes. • Heat $1/4$ cup (60 ml) of the oil in a large frying pan over low heat and sauté the anchovies until they have dissolved. • Add the cooked vegetables and sauté over high heat until lightly golden, about 3 minutes. Remove from the heat and set aside. • Sauté the onion and a little salt in 1 tablespoon of the oil in a frying pan over medium heat until softened, 3–4 minutes. • Stir in the raisins and pine nuts and sauté for 3 minutes. • Pour in the tomato paste mixture and add the parsley. Season with salt and pepper. Cook for 5 minutes more. • Toast the bread crumbs in the remaining 2 tablespoons of oil in a small frying pan over high heat for 2 minutes, until golden brown. • Cook the pasta in a large pan of salted boiling water for half the time indicated on the package. • Drain and rinse under cold running water. Drizzle with the remaining 1 tablespoon of oil to prevent sticking. • Preheat the oven to 350°F (180°C/gas 4). • Butter a large baking dish. • Arrange one-third of the pasta in the prepared baking dish. Cover with some of the sauce, sprinkle with caciocavallo, bread crumbs, almonds, and the sautéed vegetables. Make two more layers, finishing with caciocavallo and butter. • Bake for 40–45 minutes, or until the top is golden brown. • Serve hot.

12 oz (350 g) asparagus, peeled and coarsely chopped

1 lb (500 g) broccoli, separated into florets and stalks

8 oz (250 g) common or herb fennel, stalks removed and chopped

$1/2$ cup (125 ml) extra-virgin olive oil

3 salt-cured anchovies fillets

1 onion, finely chopped

Salt

2 tablespoons golden raisins (sultanas)

2 tablespoons pine nuts

1 tablespoon tomato paste (concentrate) dissolved in $3/4$ cup (200 ml) water

1 tablespoon finely chopped fresh parsley

Freshly ground black pepper

3 tablespoons fresh bread crumbs

1 lb (500 g) spaghetti or bucatini

3 oz (90 g) caciocavallo cheese, cut into small cubes, or $3/4$ cup (90 g) freshly grated pecorino cheese

$1/4$ cup (60 g) butter, cut into flakes

2 tablespoons finely chopped almonds, toasted

SERVES 4–6

PREPARATION 45 min + 1 h to chill pastry

COOKING 45–50 min

DIFFICULTY level 2

Baked Rigatoni
in a pastry crust

Pastry: Place the flour, salt, and lemon zest in a large bowl. Cut in the butter until the mixture resembles bread crumbs. Stir in the eggs. • Shape the dough into a ball, cover with plastic wrap (cling film), and refrigerate for 1 hour. • Preheat the oven to 400°F (200°C/gas 6). • Roll the dough out to ½ inch (1 cm) thick. • Butter a 9-inch (23-cm) springform pan and line with the dough. Prick with a fork. • Bake for 20 minutes, or until golden brown. • Cook the rigatoni in a large pan of salted, boiling water for half the time indicated on the package. Drain well. • Stir the rigatoni into the Béchamel and tomato sauce. • Spoon into the pastry. Sprinkle with the cheese. Bake for 15–20 minutes more. • Remove the sides from the pan and serve hot.

Pastry
2 cups (300 g) all-purpose (plain) flour
2 large egg yolks
Finely grated zest of 1 lemon
Dash of salt
½ cup (125 g) butter

1 lb (500 g) rigatoni
½ quantity Béchamel Sauce
   (see page 8)
1 quantity Tomato Sauce (see page 4)
½ cup (60 g) freshly grated Parmesan
   cheese

Baked Pasta
in a pastry crust

Mix the beef, parsley, salt, and pepper in a bowl. Shape into balls and set aside. • Heat the oil in a large frying pan over medium heat and sauté the sausage until browned. • Add the ham and mushrooms and sauté for 5 minutes. • Bring the stock to a boil. Add the meatballs and simmer for 10 minutes. Drain, reserving the stock. • Cook the pasta in a large pan of salted, boiling water until al dente. • Preheat the oven to 350°F (180°C/gas 4). • Butter an ovenproof dish and line with two-thirds of the pastry. • Spoon in half the pasta, then the sauce and remaining pasta. • Thicken 1 cup (250 ml) of the reserved stock with the flour over medium heat. Drizzle over the pie. • Cover with the remaining pastry. • Make a few holes into the top and brush with the egg yolk. • Bake for 45 minutes, or until golden brown. Serve hot.

12 oz (350 g) ground (minced) beef
2 tablespoons finely chopped fresh parsley
Salt and freshly ground black pepper
1/4 cup (60 ml) extra-virgin olive oil
8 oz (250 g) Italian sausage, crumbled
8 oz (250 g) diced ham
3 1/2 oz (100 g) dried mushrooms, soaked and chopped
4 cups (1 liter) beef stock (bouillon cube or homemade)
14 oz (400 g) rigatoni or other short, hollow pasta shape
14 oz (400 g) frozen short crust pastry, thawed and rolled
2 tablespoons all purpose (plain) flour
1 large egg yolk, beaten

27

Macaroni Pie
with pigeon and mushrooms

Set out a 9-inch (23-cm) springform pan. • Pastry: Mix the flour, sugar, and salt in a large bowl. Use a pastry blender to cut in the butter until the mixture resembles coarse crumbs. • Mix in the egg yolks and brandy to form a stiff dough, adding the water if needed. • Press the dough into a disk, wrap in plastic wrap (cling film), and refrigerate for 30 minutes. • Sauce: Heat the oil in a large saucepan over medium heat. Add the bay leaf, sage, and garlic and sauté until the garlic is pale gold, 2–3 minutes. Discard the garlic. • Increase the heat to high and add the pigeon. Sauté until browned all over, 5–7 minutes. • Pour in the wine, add the mushrooms, and simmer until the wine has evaporated. • Stir in the tomatoes and $1/4$ cup (60 ml) of stock. Season with nutmeg, salt, and pepper. • Cover and simmer over medium heat until the meat is tender, adding the remaining stock as required. • Transfer the pigeon to a cutting board and let cool completely. Remove the bones and return the meat to the pan. • Cook the pasta in salted boiling water for half the time indicated on the package. • Drain well and add to the sauce. Mix in the Parmesan and butter. • Roll out two-thirds of the pastry on a lightly floured surface to $1/4$ inch (5 mm) thick. Line the pie dish, letting the excess pastry overlap the edges. • Fill with the pasta and sauce mixture. • Roll out the remaining pastry to the size of the dish and place it on top. Brush with egg and prick all over with a fork. • Bake for 45–50 minutes, or until the pastry is golden brown. If it begins to turn dark during baking, cover with aluminum foil. • Serve hot.

Pastry
$3^1/3$ cups (500 g) all-purpose (plain) flour
$1/2$ cup (100 g) sugar
$1/2$ teaspoon salt
1 cup (250 g) butter, cut up
2 large egg yolks
2 tablespoons brandy
1–2 tablespoons cold water (optional)

Sauce
5 tablespoons extra-virgin olive oil
1 bay leaf
1 sprig fresh sage, chopped
1 clove garlic
3 pigeons or quail, each weighing about 4 oz (125 g), cleaned and quartered
$1/3$ cup (90 ml) dry red wine
1 oz (30 g) dried porcini mushrooms, soaked in warm water for 15 minutes, drained and coarsely chopped
$1/2$ cup (125 g) peeled tomatoes pressed through a fine-mesh strainer (passata)
1 cup (250 ml) beef stock (homemade or bouillon cube)
$1/8$ teaspoon freshly grated nutmeg
Salt and freshly ground white pepper
1 lb (500 g) small dried macaroni
$3/4$ cup (90 g) freshly grated Parmesan cheese
$1/4$ cup (60 g) butter, cut up
1 large egg, lightly beaten

SERVES 4–6

PREPARATION 20 min

COOKING 35 min

DIFFICULTY level 2

Baked Ravioli

with watercress and cheese

Preheat the oven to 425°F (220°C/gas 7). • Butter a baking dish. • Cook the ravioli in a large pan of salted, boiling water for 4–5 minutes, or until al dente. • Drain and set aside. • Blanch the watercress for a few seconds in salted, boiling water. Drain, run under cold water, squeeze well, and chop finely. • Mix the crescenza, Parmesan, milk, salt, and pepper in a large bowl. • Stir in the walnuts, cress, and ravioli and mix gently. • Roll the pasta dough out to very thin and line the base and sides of the prepared dish. • Spoon the ravioli mixture over the pasta. • Cover with the remaining sheet of pasta. Brush with the egg yolk and make parallel cuts in the surface. • Bake for about 20 minutes, or until the pastry is golden brown. • Let stand for 5 minutes before serving.

1 lb (500 g) ravioli with beef filling

14 oz (400 g) watercress

10 oz (300 g) crescenza or stracchino (or other fresh, creamy cheese)

½ cup (60 g) freshly grated Parmesan cheese

¾ cup (180 ml) milk

Salt and freshly ground black pepper

½ cup (50 g) finely chopped shelled walnuts

8 oz (250 g) frozen short-crust pastry, thawed

1 large egg yolk

SERVES 4–6

PREPARATION 10 min

COOKING 15 min

DIFFICULTY level 2

Radicchio Pie
with tagliatelle

Preheat the oven to 350°F (180°C/gas 4). • Slice each head of radicchio lengthwise into four and place in a baking dish. Season with salt and pepper and pour the cream over the top. • Bake for 15 minutes. • Remove from the oven and set aside. • Raise the oven temperature to 400°F (200°C/gas 6). • Butter a large baking dish. • Cook the pasta in a large pan of salted, boiling water for half the time indicated on the package. • Drain well and mix with the baked radicchio mixture and Béchamel. Place in the baking dish and sprinkle with the Parmesan. • Bake for 20–25 minutes, or until golden brown. • Serve hot.

6 heads Treviso radicchio or red chicory
Salt and freshly ground black pepper
1 cup (250 ml) heavy (double) cream
1 lb (500 g) fresh maltagliati or tagliatelle
1 quantity Béchamel Sauce (see page 8)
$^3/_4$ cup (90 g) freshly grated Parmesan cheese

SERVES 4

PREPARATION 20 min

COOKING 35 min

DIFFICULTY level 2

Baked Penne
with shrimp and salmon

Preheat the oven to 400°F (200°C/gas 6). • Sauté the onion in the oil and half the butter in a large frying pan over medium heat for 5 minutes. • Add the shrimp and salmon and sauté for 2 minutes. • Mix the cream and tomato purée in a small bowl and add to the frying pan. Season with salt and pepper, and simmer for 5 minutes. • Cook the penne in a large pot of salted, boiling water for half the time indicated on the package. Drain and place in a bowl. • Add the sauce and sprinkle with the parsley. • Butter a large sheet of aluminum foil and place the penne and their sauce in the center. Dot with the remaining butter and fold the foil over to seal. • Bake for 15 minutes. • When cooked, arrange on a heated serving dish. Serve at once, opening the foil package on the table.

1 medium onion, finely chopped

2 tablespoons extra-virgin olive oil

1/4 cup (60 g) butter

4 oz (125 g) shrimp, shelled and coarsely chopped

4 oz (125 g) smoked salmon, coarsely chopped

1/3 cup (90 ml) light (single) cream

3 tablespoons tomato concentrate (paste)

Salt and freshly ground black pepper

1 lb (500 g) penne

3 tablespoons finely chopped fresh parsley

34

SERVES 4–6

PREPARATION 15 min

COOKING 30 min

DIFFICULTY level 1

Baked Frittata

with tagliatelle

Preheat the oven to 400°F (200°C/gas 6). • Heat the oil in a small frying pan and sauté the shallots over low heat for 10 minutes. • Cook the pasta in a large pan of salted, boiling water for half the time indicated on the package. • Meanwhile, beat the eggs in a large bowl with the Parmesan, parsley, salt, and nutmeg. • Drain the pasta well and add to the bowl with the eggs. • Add the shallots and transfer the mixture to an oiled 9-inch (23-cm) springform pan. • Bake for 20 minutes, or until golden brown. • Serve hot or at room temperature.

2 tablespoons extra-virgin olive oil

4 shallots, finely chopped

1 lb (500 g) dried tagliatelle

4 large eggs

1 cup (125 g) freshly grated Parmesan cheese

1 tablespoon finely chopped fresh parsley

Freshly grated nutmeg

Salt

Baked Tomatoes
with pasta filling

Rinse the tomatoes and dry well. Cut the top third off each tomato (with its stalk) and set aside. Hollow out the insides of the bottom parts with a teaspoon. Put the pulp in a bowl. • Place a basil leaf in the bottom of each hollow shell. • Preheat the oven to 350°F (180°C/gas 4). • Cook the pasta in a medium pot of salted, boiling water for half the time indicated on the package. Drain well. • Combine the pasta with the tomato pulp. Add the parsley and 2 tablespoons of the oil. Season with salt and pepper. • Stuff the hollow tomatoes with the mixture. • Grease an ovenproof dish with the remaining oil and carefully place the tomatoes on it. Cover each tomato with its top. • Bake for about 40–45 minutes, or until the tomatoes are tender and the pasta is fully cooked. • Serve hot or at room temperature.

8 medium tomatoes
8 basil leaves
2 tablespoons finely chopped fresh parsley
3 tablespoons extra-virgin olive oil
Salt and freshly ground black pepper
8 tablespoons ditaloni rigati or other small, tubular pasta

Baked Pasta
with chicken and truffles

Sauté the onion in 2 tablespoons of butter in a saucepan over medium heat until softened, 3–4 minutes. • Add the tomato paste mixture and season with salt and pepper. • Sauté the chicken and veal in ¼ cup (60 g) of butter in a frying pan over high heat until browned, 5–7 minutes. Preheat the oven to 400°F (200°C/gas 6). • Butter a baking dish. • Process the chicken, veal, and ham with ½ cup (125 ml) of cream and the truffles in a food processor until smooth. • Cook the pasta in a large pot of salted boiling water for half the time indicated on the package. Drain and run under cold water to cool. • Using a pastry bag, fill the pasta with the meat mixture. • Transfer half the filled pasta to the prepared dish. Top with the onion sauce and dot with 3 tablespoons of butter. Sprinkle with ¼ cup (30 g) of cheese. • Place the remaining filled pasta on top and cover with the remaining ¼ cup (60 ml) cream. Top with the remaining butter and cheese. • Bake for 15–20 minutes, or until golden brown.
Serve hot.

1 onion, thinly sliced
⅔ cup (180 g) butter
1 tablespoon tomato paste (concentrate) mixed with ¼ cup (60 ml) beef stock
Salt and freshly ground black pepper
5 oz (150 g) boneless, skinless chicken breast, chopped
5 oz (150 g) veal, chopped
8 oz (250 g) ham, thickly sliced
¾ cup (180 ml) heavy (double) cream
½ oz (15 g) black truffles
12 oz (350 g) large dried smooth or ridged tube pasta
¾ cup (90 g) freshly grated Gruyière (Swiss) cheese

SERVES 6–8

PREPARATION 30 min + 1 h to drain

COOKING 5 min

DIFFICULTY level 2

Baked Bucatini
with sardines and eggplant

Put the eggplant in a colander and sprinkle with salt. Let drain for 1 hour. • Heat the frying oil in a large frying pan until very hot. • Fry the eggplants in small batches until golden brown, 5–7 minutes. • Drain on paper towels. • Sauté the garlic in 5 tablespoons of extra-virgin olive oil in a large frying pan over medium heat until pale gold. • Stir in the tomatoes and season with salt and pepper. Simmer for 5 minutes, until the tomatoes have broken down. • Add the sardines to the sauce. Simmer over low heat for 10 minutes. • Cook the pasta in a large pot of salted boiling water until al dente. • Drain well. • Preheat the oven to 400°F (200°C/gas 6). • Grease a baking dish with the remaining extra-virgin olive oil and sprinkle with bread crumbs. • Layer the pasta, sardine sauce, fried eggplant, and half the pecorino in the baking dish. • Cover with the remaining pecorino, oregano, salt, pepper, and bread crumbs. • Bake for 10–15 minutes, or until lightly golden. Serve hot.

2 medium eggplants (aubergines), thinly sliced

Coarse sea salt

1 cup (250 ml) olive oil, for frying

1/3 cup (90 ml) extra-virgin olive oil

2 cloves garlic, finely chopped

1 cup (250 ml) peeled and chopped tomatoes

Salt and freshly ground black pepper

1 lb (500 g) fresh sardines, cleaned and chopped

1 lb (500 g) bucatini

4 tablespoons fine dry bread crumbs

6 tablespoons freshly grated pecorino cheese

1 teaspoon finely chopped fresh oregano

Baked Tagliatelle
with shrimp and white wine

Preheat the oven to 400°F (200°C/gas 6). • Butter a large baking dish. • Cook the shrimp in 4 cups (1 liter) of boiling water for 2–3 minutes. Remove with a slotted spoon. Use a pair of sharply pointed scissors to cut down the center of their backs. Pull the sides of the shell apart and take out the flesh, keeping it as intact as possible, and set aside. • Return the shells and heads to the stock and continue boiling until reduced by two-thirds. • Heat the oil and ¼ cup (60 g) of butter in a frying pan over medium heat. Add the garlic and onion and sauté until softened, 3–4 minutes. • Add the shrimp flesh. Sprinkle with the wine and simmer until evaporated. Season with salt. Remove from the heat. • Melt the remaining butter in a small saucepan. Stir in the flour and keep stirring to prevent lumps forming as you add first the hot milk and then the strained hot stock. Cook, stirring constantly, until the sauce is thickened, 7–10 minutes. • Cook the pasta in a large pan of salted, boiling water until al dente. • Drain and add to the frying pan with the shrimp mixture. Pour in the sauce and stir gently over low heat. Transfer to the prepared baking dish. Sprinkle with the Parmesan and parsley. Bake for 10–15 minutes, or until golden brown on top. Serve hot.

1¼ lb (600 g) shrimp
1 clove garlic, finely chopped
1 small onion, finely chopped
3 tablespoons extra-virgin olive oil
⅓ cup (90 g) butter
½ cup (125 ml) dry white wine
Salt
3 tablespoons all-purpose (plain) flour
1 cup (250 ml) hot milk
1 lb (500 g) tagliatelle
1 cup (125 g) freshly grated Parmesan cheese
2 tablespoons finely chopped fresh parsley

SERVES 4–6

PREPARATION 1 h + 1 h to soak

COOKING 45 min

DIFFICULTY level 2

Baked Spaghetti
with seafood

Soak the clams and mussels in separate large bowls of warm salted water for 1 hour. • Drain and set aside. Scrub any beards off the mussels. • Cook the clams and mussels separately (or one at a time) in a large frying pan over high heat, shaking the pan often, until they have all opened. Discard any that have not opened. • Remove most of the mollusks from their shells, leaving just a few to garnish the dish. • Cut the squid's bodies into rounds and the tentacles in pieces. • Preheat the oven to 350°F (180°C/gas 4). • Heat the oil in a large frying pan and sauté the garlic, chile, and parsley until the garlic is pale gold. • Pour in the wine and cook until it evaporates. • Stir in the tomatoes and cook for 5 minutes. • Add the squid, clams, mussels, and shrimp. Cover and cook over high heat for 10 minutes. • Cook the spaghetti in salted, boiling water for half the time indicated on the package. Reserve the cooking water. • Drain and add to the pan with the sauce. • Cut four to six large pieces of aluminum foil and fold each in half to double the thickness. • Divide the pasta into four to six portions and place in the center of the pieces of foil, adding 3 tablespoons of the cooking water from the pasta to each portion. Close, sealing the foil well. There should be an air pocket in each of the packages. • Transfer to a large baking sheet. • Bake for 12–15 minutes, or until the parcels have puffed up slightly. • Serve the parcels, still closed, on individual plates.

1½ lb (750 g) clams, in shell
1½ lb (750 g) mussels, in shell
14 oz (400 g) squid, cleaned
⅓ cup (90 ml) extra-virgin olive oil
2 cloves garlic, finely chopped
1 dried red chile pepper, crumbled
2 tablespoons finely chopped fresh parsley
½ cup (125 ml) dry white wine
1 lb (500 g) firm-ripe tomatoes, peeled, seeded, and thinly sliced
12 oz (350 g) shrimp
1 lb (500 g) spaghetti

Fresh Cannelloni
with meat sauce

Meat Sauce: Sauté the pancetta in the oil in a Dutch oven (casserole) over medium heat for 5 minutes. • Add the beef, onion, celery, garlic, parsley, cinnamon, rosemary, and bay leaf. • Pour in the wine and the tomatoes and basil. Season with salt and pepper and bring to a boil. Cover and simmer over low heat for 2 hours, or until the meat is tender, adding water if the sauce begins to stick to the pan. • Discard the cinnamon stick, rosemary, and bay leaf. • Remove from the heat and process the meat with 3 tablespoons of the cooking juices in a food processor until chopped. • Pasta Dough: Sift the flour and salt into a mound on a work surface and make a well in the center. Mix in the egg yolks and enough water to make a smooth dough. Knead until smooth and elastic, 15–20 minutes. • Shape the dough into a ball, wrap in plastic wrap (cling film), and let rest for 30 minutes. • Roll out the dough on a lightly floured surface until thin. Cut into 6 x 8-inch (15 x 20-cm) strips. • Preheat the oven to 375°F (190°C/gas 5). • Butter a large baking dish. • Blanch the pieces of dough for 1 minute each and lay on a damp cloth. • Spread the meat sauce over the pasta and roll up carefully into rolls from the long side. • Arrange the cannelloni in a baking dish and cover with the meat sauce. • Beat the eggs with the salt and pepper and 2 tablespoons cheese. Sprinkle the remaining cheese over the meat sauce. Pour the eggs over the top. • Bake for 30–35 minutes, or until the top is brown. Serve hot.

Meat Sauce
3/4 cup (100 g) diced pancetta
1/3 cup (90 ml) extra-virgin olive oil
1 lb (500 g) stewing beef, in a single piece
1 red onion, chopped
1 stalk celery, chopped
2 cloves garlic, chopped
2 tablespoons finely chopped fresh parsley
1 stick cinnamon
1 sprig rosemary
1 bay leaf
1/4 cup (60 ml) red wine
3 lb (1.5 kg) peeled plum tomatoes, pressed through a fine mesh strainer (passata)
1 sprig fresh basil
Salt and freshly ground black pepper
Hot water, as required

Pasta Dough
2²/₃ cups (300 g) all-purpose (plain) flour
1/4 teaspoon salt
3 large egg yolks
Lukewarm water

Topping
2 large eggs
Salt and freshly ground black pepper
1¹/₂ cups (200 g) freshly grated caciocavallo or ricotta salata cheese

SERVES 4–6

PREPARATION 45 min

COOKING 35 min

DIFFICULTY level 2

Cannelloni
with spinach and meat sauce

Preheat the oven to 400°F (200°C/gas 6). • Butter a large baking dish. • Cook the cannelloni in a large pan of salted, boiling water for half the time indicated on the package. Drain and lay on a clean cloth. • Finely chop the roast beef, spinach, and prosciutto in a food processor and transfer to large bowl. Mix in the eggs and half the Parmesan. Season with salt, pepper, and nutmeg. • Fill the cannelloni with the filling and arrange them in layers in the baking dish. Cover each layer with meat sauce. Top with Béchamel sauce. Dot with the butter and sprinkle with Parmesan. • Bake for 15–20 minutes, or until golden brown. • Let stand for 5 minutes before serving.

12 oz (350 g) dried cannelloni
14 oz (400 g) cooked roast beef
3 oz (100 g) cooked, drained spinach
5 oz (150 g) prosciutto (Parma ham)
2 large eggs
8 tablespoons freshly grated Parmesan cheese
Salt and freshly ground black pepper
1/4 teaspoon freshly grated nutmeg
1 quantity Meat Sauce (see page 7)
1 quantity Béchamel Sauce (see page 8)
1 tablespoon butter, cut into flakes

SERVES 4

PREPARATION 1 h

COOKING 2 h

DIFFICULTY level 2

Lasagne
with meatballs

Meat Sauce: Heat the oil in a large saucepan over medium heat. Add the beef and ham and sauté for 3–4 minutes, until browned all over. • Pour in the wine and let it evaporate for about 3 minutes. • Stir in the tomato sauce and season with salt and pepper. Cook over low heat for at least 1 hour. • Preheat the oven to 400°F (200°C/gas 6). • Oil a baking dish. • Meatballs: Mix the veal, eggs, and pecorino in a large bowl. Season with salt and pepper and form into balls the size of hazelnuts. • Add the meatballs to the meat sauce and cook for 10 minutes. • Blanch the lasagne sheets in small batches in a large pan of salted boiling water with 1 tablespoon of oil. Scoop out with a slotted spoon, squeeze gently, and let dry on a clean cloth. • Lay the first layer of lasagne in the baking dish. Cover with a layer of meat sauce, mozzarella, hard-boiled eggs, and pecorino. Continue to layer the ingredients for a total of five layers. Dot with the butter and sprinkle with any remaining pecorino. • Bake for 35–40 minutes, or until golden brown. • Let rest 10 minutes before serving.

Meat Sauce
2 tablespoons extra-virgin olive oil
8 oz (250 g) lean ground (minced) beef
4 oz (125 g) ham, finely chopped
1/3 cup (90 ml) dry red wine
1 quantity Tomato Sauce (see page 4)
Salt and freshly ground black pepper

Meatballs
12 oz (300 g) ground (minced) beef
2 large eggs
2 tablespoons freshly grated pecorino cheese

12 oz (300 g) lasagne sheets
8 oz (250 g) fresh mozzarella cheese, sliced
3 hard-boiled eggs, finely chopped
3/4 cup (90 g) freshly grated pecorino cheese
2 tablespoons butter, cut into flakes

SERVES 6

PREPARATION 45 min + 30 min to rest

COOKING 3 h

DIFFICULTY level 3

Classic Lasagne

Pasta Dough: Sift the flour and salt into a mound on a work surface and make a well in the center. Break in the eggs and mix with a fork to make a dough. Knead the dough for 15–20 minutes, until smooth and elastic. Shape into a ball, wrap in plastic wrap, (cling film) and let rest for 30 minutes. • Roll out the dough on a lightly floured surface until paper-thin. Cut into 6 x 8-inch (15 x 20-cm) rectangles. Alternatively, roll out the dough using a pasta machine. • Blanch the lasagne sheets in small batches in a large pan of salted boiling water with 1 tablespoon of oil. Scoop out with a slotted spoon, squeeze gently, and let dry on a clean cloth. • Meat Sauce: Sauté the prosciutto, onion, celery, and carrot in the butter in a large frying pan over medium heat until browned, about 5 minutes. • Add the beef and cook for 2–3 minutes until browned all over. • Pour in the wine and let it evaporate. • Stir in the tomatoes and $\frac{1}{2}$ cup (125 ml) of stock. Season with salt, cover, and cook over low heat for about 2 hours, adding more stock if needed. Season with salt and pepper. • Preheat the oven to 400°F (200°C/gas 6). • Butter a baking dish. • Arrange four layers of pasta in the prepared dish, alternating with meat sauce, Béchamel, and Parmesan. • Bake for 20–25 minutes, or until bubbling. Serve warm.

Pasta Dough
2 cups (300 g) all-purpose (plain) flour
$\frac{1}{4}$ teaspoon salt
3 large eggs

Meat Sauce
5 oz (150 g) prosciutto (Parma ham), chopped
1 onion, chopped
1 stalk celery, chopped
1 carrot, finely chopped
$\frac{1}{4}$ cup (60 g) butter
8 oz (250 g) ground (minced) beef
$\frac{1}{3}$ cup (90 ml) dry white wine
1 cup (250 g) chopped tomatoes
$\frac{1}{2}$ cup (125 ml) beef stock + more as needed
Salt and freshly ground black pepper
1 quantity Béchamel Sauce (see page 8)
$\frac{3}{4}$ cup (90 g) freshly grated Parmesan cheese

Seafood Lasagne

If using homemade pasta, prepare it following the instructions on page 48. • Blanch the lasagne sheets in small batches in a large pan of salted boiling water with 1 tablespoon of oil. Scoop out with a slotted spoon, squeeze gently, and let dry on a clean cloth. • Heat the remaining oil in a large frying pan over medium heat and sauté the garlic and half the parsley until the garlic is pale gold, about 3 minutes. • Pour in the wine and simmer until it evaporates. • Add the squid and sauté over high heat for 5 minutes. Add the shrimp, shellfish, and fish. Season with salt and pepper and simmer over medium heat for 5 minutes. Add the remaining parsley and remove from the heat. • Preheat the oven to 350°F (180°C/gas 4). • Butter a large baking dish. • Melt the butter in a medium saucepan and stir in the flour. Pour in the stock and simmer, stirring constantly, until thickened, 7–10 minutes. • Arrange a layer of pasta in the prepared dish. Spread with a layer of fish sauce and cover with a layer of fish cream. Repeat until all the ingredients are in the dish. • Bake until golden brown, 20–30 minutes. • Let rest for 10 minutes before serving.

1 quantity lasagne (see page 48) or 12 oz (350 g) fresh storebought lasagne sheets
5 tablespoons extra-virgin olive oil
2 cloves garlic, finely chopped
2 tablespoons finely chopped parsley
1/2 cup (125 ml) dry white wine
12 oz (350 g) squid, cleaned and chopped
12 oz (350 g) shrimp (prawn) tails, shelled and deveined
12 oz (350 g) mixed clams and mussels, shelled
14 oz (400 g) firm-textured fish fillets, chopped
Salt and freshly ground white pepper
1/3 cup (90 g) butter
1/2 cup (75 g) all-purpose (plain) flour
4 cups (1 liter) fish stock

SERVES 4–6

PREPARATION 90 min + 30 min to rest

COOKING 40 min

DIFFICULTY level 3

Sweet Lasagne
with poppy seeds

Pasta Dough: Sift both flours and salt into a mound a work surface and make a well in the center. Mix in the eggs, oil, and enough water to make a smooth dough. Knead for 15–20 minutes, until smooth and elastic. Shape into a ball, wrap in plastic wrap (cling film), and let rest for 30 minutes. • Filling: Chop one apple into small cubes and cut the remaining apple into thin slices. Place the apple cubes and slices in separate bowls of water and lemon juice. Let stand 15 minutes. Drain well. • Mix the apple cubes, figs, raisins, and walnuts. • Preheat the oven to 325°F (170°C/gas 3). • Butter a baking dish. • Roll out the dough out on a lightly floured work surface until paper-thin. Cut into ³⁄₄ x 3-inch (2 x 8-cm) rectangles. • Blanch the lasagne sheets in small batches in a large pan of salted boiling water with 1 tablespoon of oil. Scoop out with a slotted spoon, squeeze gently, and let dry on a clean cloth. • Layer the pasta in the dish with the apple mixture. • Drizzle with ¹⁄₃ cup (90 g) of the butter. • Drain the apple slices and arrange on the pasta. • Drizzle with the remaining butter and sprinkle with the poppy seeds and cinnamon. • Bake for 25–30 minutes, or until the apple has softened. • Let rest for 10 minutes before serving.

Pasta Dough
1¹⁄₃ cups (200 g) durum wheat flour
1¹⁄₃ cups (200 g) all-purpose (plain) flour
¹⁄₄ teaspoon salt
2 large eggs + 1 large egg yolk
1 tablespoon extra-virgin olive oil
1 tablespoon water + more if needed

Filling
2 tart apples, such as Granny Smiths
Freshly squeezed juice of ¹⁄₂ lemon
Generous ¹⁄₄ cup (50 g) dried figs, coarsely chopped
2 tablespoons raisins, plumped in warm water for 1 hour
1 cup (100 g) coarsely chopped walnuts
²⁄₃ cup (150 g) butter, melted
¹⁄₂ teaspoon ground cinnamon
¹⁄₄ cup (50 g) poppy seeds

Neapolitan Lasagne

If using homemade pasta, prepare it following the instructions on page 48. • Blanch the lasagne sheets in small batches in a large pan of salted boiling water with 1 tablespoon of oil. Scoop out with a slotted spoon, squeeze gently, and let dry on a clean cloth. • Heat the butter in a large frying pan over medium heat. Add the onion and beef and sauté until lightly browned, 5–7 minutes. Season with salt and pepper and add the tomatoes. Simmer over medium-low heat for 1 hour, adding stock gradually to keep moist. • When the meat is cooked, remove from the frying pan and chop finely in a food processor. Reserve the sauce. • Transfer the chopped meat to a mixing bowl and add the parsley, egg and half the Parmesan. Shape the mixture into small meatballs. • Heat the oil in a large frying pan and fry the meatballs for 8–10 minutes, or until nicely browned. Drain on paper towels. • Preheat the oven to 350°F (180°C/gas 4). • Butter an ovenproof dish and cover the bottom with a layer of lasagne, followed by layers of salami, mozzarella, ham, Parmesan, meatballs and sauce. Repeat until all the ingredients are in the dish. Finish with a layer of Parmesan. • Bake for 20 minutes, or until golden brown. • Set aside for a few minutes before serving.

1 quantity lasagne (see page 48) or 12 oz (350 g) fresh storebought lasagne sheets

$^1/_3$ cup (90 g) butter

1 onion, finely chopped

12 oz (300 g) beef loin, in 1 piece

Salt and freshly ground black pepper

1 (14-oz/400-g) can tomatoes, chopped, with juice

$^1/_2$ cup (125 ml) beef stock (homemade or bouillon cube)

2 tablespoons finely chopped fresh parsley

1 large egg

1 cup (125 g) freshly grated Parmesan cheese

1 cup (250 ml) olive oil, for frying

4 oz (125 g) salami, cut in cubes

12 oz (350 g) mozzarella cheese, cut in small cubes

4 oz (125 g) prosciutto (Parma ham), cut in cubes

SERVES 4–6

PREPARATION 30 min + 1 h for the pasta

COOKING 1 h 30 min

DIFFICULTY level 2

Lasagne
with mushrooms

If using homemade pasta, prepare it following the instructions on page 48. • Blanch the lasagne sheets in small batches in a large pan of salted boiling water with 1 tablespoon of oil. Scoop out with a slotted spoon, squeeze gently, and let dry on a clean cloth. • Preheat the oven to 400°F (200°C/gas 6). • Sauté the carrots, celery, and shallots in the oil in a large frying pan over medium heat for 5–6 minutes. • Add the meat and cook, stirring often, for 10 minutes. • Add the tomatoes and simmer for 20 minutes. • Stir in the mushrooms and simmer for 20 minutes more. • Remove from the heat. Stir in the prosciutto and season with the salt and pepper. • Spoon a layer of meat into an ovenproof dish. Cover with a layer of pasta. Top with a layer of Fontina and sprinkle with the Parmesan. Repeat until the dish is full. Finish with a cheese layer. • Bake for 25–30 minutes, or until golden brown. • Let rest for 5 minutes before serving.

1 quantity lasagne (see page 48) or 12 oz (350 g) fresh storebought lasagne sheets

1 carrot, finely chopped

2 stalks celery, finely chopped

2 shallots, finely chopped

1/4 cup (60 ml) extra-virgin olive oil

8 oz (250 g) ground (minced) beef

14 oz (400 g) chopped tomatoes

1 lb (500 g) porcini or white mushrooms, finely chopped

1/2 cup (75 g) finely chopped prosciutto (Parma ham)

Salt and freshly ground black pepper

8 oz (250 g) sliced Fontina cheese

1 cup (125 g) freshly grated Parmesan cheese

Pizzoccheri

with cabbage and cheese

Combine both flours in a large bowl. Add the eggs, milk, and salt and stir to obtain a firm dough. • Place on a lightly floured work surface and knead until smooth and elastic, about 15 minutes. Set aside for 30 minutes. • Roll the pasta out until about $\frac{1}{4}$ inch (3 mm) thick. Roll the sheet of pasta loosely and cut into strips $\frac{1}{2}$ inch (1 cm) wide and 3 inches (8 cm) long. • Preheat the oven to 350°F (180°C/gas 4). • Chop the potatoes in $\frac{1}{2}$ inch (1 cm) cubes and chop the cabbage into strips. • Bring a large saucepan of lightly salted water to a boil and cook the potatoes and cabbage. Put the potatoes in 5 minutes before the cabbage. • When the potatoes are almost cooked, add the pasta. • When the vegetables and pasta are cooked, drain carefully. • Melt the butter with the garlic and sage in a small saucepan. Cook for 2 minutes. • Butter an ovenproof dish. • Place a layer of pasta in the bottom of the dish and cover with a layer of potato and cabbage. Drizzle with a little butter, sprinkle with pepper and Parmesan, and cover with slices of Fontina. Repeat this layering process two or three times until all the ingredients are in the dish. Finish with a layer of Parmesan. • Bake for 25 minutes, or until golden brown on top. Serve hot.

$2\frac{1}{2}$ cups (375 g) buckwheat flour

$1\frac{1}{2}$ cups (225 g) all-purpose (plain) flour

3 large eggs

$\frac{1}{2}$ cup (125 ml) milk

1 teaspoon salt

8 oz (250 g) potatoes

6 oz (180 g) Savoy cabbage

$\frac{2}{3}$ cup (150 g) butter

2 cloves garlic, finely chopped

4 leaves fresh sage

Fresh ground black pepper to taste

1 cup (125 g) freshly grated Parmesan cheese

6 oz (180 g) Fontina cheese, thinly sliced

Pasta Roll
with zucchini filling

Melt 2 tablespoons of butter in a large frying pan over medium heat and sauté the zucchini until golden. • Add the flowers, sauté for 1 minute, then remove from the heat. • Mix the robiola, zucchini, flowers, half the Parmesan, salt, and pepper in a large bowl. • Blanch the lasagne sheets in a large pan of salted boiling water with 1 tablespoon of oil. Scoop out with a slotted spoon, squeeze gently, and let dry on a clean cloth. • Preheat the oven to 350°F (180°C/gas 4). • Transfer each lasagne sheet to a piece of buttered parchment paper. Spread the cheese and zucchini mixture over the pasta and roll up. Wrap in the paper and tie the ends with string. Bake for 10 minutes. • Heat the oil in a large frying pan and sauté the garlic until pale gold. Remove from heat and add the basil. Discard the garlic. • Slice the baked rolls and sprinkle with the remaining Parmesan. Top with the pine nuts and basil sauce. • Bake for 5 minutes.

½ cup (60 ml) butter, cut up

10 oz (300 g) zucchini (courgettes), cut in thin strips

8 zucchini (courgette) flowers, chopped

8 oz (250 g) robiola or other fresh, creamy cheese

½ cup (60 g) freshly grated Parmesan cheese

Salt and freshly ground black pepper

3 large fresh lasagne sheets

5 tablespoons extra-virgin olive oil

1 clove garlic, crushed but whole

8 leaves basil, torn

2 tablespoons pine nuts, toasted

Lasagne
with prosciutto and peas

If using homemade pasta, prepare it following the instructions on page 48. • Blanch the lasagne sheets in small batches in a large pan of salted boiling water with 1 tablespoon of oil. Scoop out with a slotted spoon, squeeze gently, and let dry on a clean cloth. • Preheat the oven to 350°F (180°C/gas 4). • Butter an ovenproof baking dish. • Melt 3 tablespoons of butter in a large frying pan and sauté the prosciutto and onion for 5 minutes. • Stir in the peas and cook for 3 minutes. Pour in the cream and season with salt and pepper. Cook over medium heat for 5 minutes. • Remove from the heat and add the basil. • Arrange a layer of lasagne in the prepared dish. Top with peas and prosciutto and sprinkle with Parmesan. Repeat until all the ingredients are in the dish, finishing with Parmesan. • Bake for 10–15 minutes, or until golden brown. • Serve hot.

1 quantity lasagne (see page 48) or 12 oz (350 g) fresh storebought lasagne sheets
5 tablespoons butter
3 oz (90 g) prosciutto (Parma ham), cut in strips
1 small onion, finely chopped
2$\frac{1}{2}$ cups (350 g) cooked peas
1 cup (250 ml) heavy (double) cream
Salt and freshly ground black pepper
1 small bunch fresh basil, torn
1 cup (125 g) freshly grated Parmesan cheese

Tagliatelle Cake

Pastry: Sift the flour into a large bowl and add the butter, confectioners' sugar, egg yolks, lemon zest, and salt. Mix rapidly with your hands and shape into a ball. Wrap in plastic wrap (cling film) and refrigerate for 30 minutes. • Place a large pan of water over high heat with the coarse sea salt. Cover and bring to a boil. • Preheat the oven to 400°F (200°C/gas 6). • Roll the pastry out on a lightly floured work surface. Place in an 8-inch (20-cm) round springform pan and prick well a fork. • Cover the pastry with aluminum foil and fill with pie weights or dried beans. • Bake for 15–20 minutes, or until pale golden brown. Remove from the oven and let cool. Remove the pie weights or beans and foil. • Filling: Soak the sultanas, pine nuts, and citron peel in a small bowl with the rum or brandy. • In a separate bowl, beat the egg yolks with the sugar until pale and creamy. Beat in the milk or cream. • Cook the tagliatelle in the boiling water for 2 minutes. Drain well and mix with the egg and sugar mixture and dried fruit. Mix well and spoon into the precooked pastry shell. • Bake for 30 minutes, or until the filling mixture is dried out. • Serve warm or at room temperature.

Pastry
2 cups (300 g) all-purpose (plain) flour
1/2 cup (125 g) cold butter, cut up
3/4 cup (125 g) confectioners' (icing) sugar
3 large egg yolks
Finely grated zest of 1/2 lemon
Pinch of salt

Filling
4 tablespoons golden raisins (sultanas)
4 tablespoons pine nuts
3 tablespoons candied citron peel, cut in small cubes
3 tablespoons rum or brandy
3 large egg yolks
6 tablespoons sugar
2–3 tablespoons milk or cream
Salt

8 oz (250 g) fresh tagliatelle

Index

Baked Pasta

was created and produced by McRae Books Srl

Via del Salviatino 1 – 50016 Fiesole, (Florence) Italy

info@mcraebooks.com

Publishers: Anne McRae and Marco Nardi

Project Director: Anne McRae

Design: Sara Mathews

Texts: McRae Books archive

Editing: Carla Bardi

Photography: Studio Lanza (Lorenzo Borri, Cristina Canepari, Ke-ho Casati, Mauro Corsi, Gil Gallo, Leonardo Pasquinelli, Gianni Petronio, Stefano Pratesi, Sandra Preussinger)

Home Economist: Benedetto Rillo

Artbuying: McRae Books

Layouts: Aurora Granata, Filippo Delle Monache, Davide Gasparri

Repro: Fotolito Raf, Florence

ISBN 978-88-6098-085-4

Printed and bound in China